Of Gods And Heroes

Written And Published By

Daf Richards

Other Books:

ISBN: 0-9539113-6-5

This book is dedicated to my granddaughters
Gemma and Rebecca.

Paragon

Tom - my darling angel cat
has flown to another place.
He no longer sits and chats
or puts a smile upon my face.
I miss his caring friendship
and all the love he gave.
I even miss those playful nips,
for now he's in his grave.

His spirit soars with heroes,
his heart lies with the slain,
he bites the hand of Nero
who has just reached Heavens plain.
He loves those little children
whose young lives did not last,
and he whispers to the tiny wren
he would've tortured in the past.

And now he sees the hand of God
in everything that grows.
The mighty trees, the grassy sod,
and the snowy cold ice floes.

A Rose

A rose is perfect.
It comes from Heavens garden.
Its scent wafts on clouds
and fills the world with beauty
that endures eternally.

Animal Heaven

At night when I lay down to sleep
to rest my busy mind.
My body languid in repose,
my stressful day behind.

My spirit's freed, it floats away
and soars up with the birds,
glides with the mighty eagle
and rides the jungle herds.

Then it dives into the ocean
and swims with all the whales,
visits Neptunes grotto
and drifts amidst the sails.

It races with the wolf pack
and listens to their song,
which tells of all their troubles,
for the human race is wrong.

It hears the leopard calling
and the lions roaring loud.
It meets the glorious tiger
then it floats into the clouds.

My spirit does this every night
while I am in my bed.
It fills my heart with happiness
which lingers in my head.

Then when I go to work next day
I'm calm and I'm serene,
for I'm a part of all those animals
which I have truly seen.

Athena Kamiras

Athena, Goddess of wisdom
rules her city in the sun
with kindness and aplomb,
smiling at her peoples fun.
She knows their faults,
forgives their weaknesses,
looks down from Heavens vaults
and heals their sicknesses.
She fought for that city,
gave it all her strength.
The women she made pretty
and to the men gave length.
This place of wondrous beauty,
of olive groves rich booty.

Haiku

The Queen of Heaven,
Hera sees her planet weep
for its dead children.

Avarice

The greed of so many humans
who live on planet earth,
decimates vast populations
who dwell inside its girth.

There's whales, seals and dolphins,
and cod and tuna too.
There's walruses and sea cows
to name but a precious few.

There's eagles, robins, blackbirds,
and songbirds, gulls and wrens,
and chickens, pheasants, turkeys,
who're bred to feed our men.

There's tigers, leopards, lions,
gorillas and chimpanzees.
Wolves and bears and bullocks,
who from man would like to flee.

And lastly, there are our own kind,
who we beat and put in chains,
and starve and maim and kill
to add to our own cruel gains.

Perhaps this is the worst thing
for animals don't torture each other,
but we march on - driven by hatred
t'wards our sisters and our brothers.

We want it *all*, everything there is,
no matter to whom it belongs to,
we'll make it all ours, take what we want,
without caring who we do the wrong to.

And yet - deep inside of us all
there's a soul that yearns for peace,
that knows what we do is not right,
that eventually *all* wars will cease.

For war is a sin, we'll discover that soon,
and then we will better our lives,
we'll love all the species that live in this world
and forget all our greedy old drives.

Then the planet will shine, the people will glow
and the world will be happy indeed,
we will open our hearts, call everything friend
and drive out that destroying creed.

Bran The Blessed

Bran the Blessed oversees the eternal
battle between the Red Dragon of Wales,
who fights with unceasing regularity
the White Dragon of England for dominion,
supremacy and old time Pagan purity.

Fairylands hosts watch from Irelands sidhs
the Shamatic shape shifting in limen space.
Calling of Wyverns, forging of Nations,
with the ageless Grail renewing life,
defeating death, maladies and starvation.

The White hounds of the Soul hunter
with their blood red eyes, see that
which is hidden deep down inside.
They howl mournfully as they race
along chasing what will be denied.

So much is lost from time, so many things
that existed and are now called Myths.
If we only knew how to use these Legends,
we could progress forwards through time
reviving our ancient knowledge trends.

We could travel on Dragons wings to the
ends of the Universe. Right wrongs, heal
planets, fill our hearts with love
for beings of every kind, every face.
We could dance on the stars above!

Bridge Of Dreams

Pegasus stands on the bridge of dreams
which crosses the glorious clouds.
He surveys the world and majestic wings
fly him high o'er the chattering crowds.

His snow white body, lithe and strong
will carry the ills of mankind,
and the purity that's in his heart
will bring out the tie that binds.

So ride on Pegasus whene'er you can
and dream all your favourite dreams,
then leap right over the setting sun
and bathe in its radiant beams.

Two Haiku

Apollon, God of
sunshine, light and music, plays
his golden syrinx.

Poseidon strides from
the depths to Kamiras and
warns of Spartan ships.

City In The Sea

Venice - city of marbled glory,
gondolas glide down the canals,
majestic, towering buildings
throw shadows over the water.

St Marks square, the cathedral,
the tower, the pavement cafes,
pigeons pecking at the crumbs,
men walking with their daughters.

The Doges palace, bridge of sighs,
water taxis, water buses,
glass works, jewellers, tourists,
the endless luggage porters.

This is the Ruby of Italy,
where life is lived richly,
where girls glow with beauty
and love never falters.

Hove Beach

Hove beach in 1824,
women wear long dresses
and white houses watch
boats with brown sails.
Waves ripple gently,
white crests hit the beach,
dark clouds hide the sun
and the wind blows high.

Dervaig

Dervaig's like a picture postcard
with sheep wand'ring o'er the hills.
Grey seals swim round the coastline,
otters play in tinkling rills.

Dervaig has the tiniest of theatres,
with forty three seats in the place.
Superb acting's performed nightly,
each seat holds an enraptured face.

Dervaig has sea life surveys every summer,
people count the whales and sharks,
then watch seabirds in their thousands,
it's a giant wildlife park!

Loch Na Keal

Loch na Keal, Isle of Mull.
Dramatic skies and louring waters.
Mountains, rocks, grass, peace,
and flowers gilding an ancient hull.

Haiku

We must destroy all
evil things, evil people
and evil spirits.

Disquiet

The stars shine in the sky
and galaxies spiral and twirl.
The wise ones gave them the names
of animals or men or girls.
There's Ursa Major and Minor,
Polaris - steady and true,
which guides our sailors at night
when the moon has hidden the blue
of the great and glorious Heaven
which covers our world like a sheet.
It protects and guards our people
until in the morning they meet
with all the hustle and bustle
that daybreak and sunshine can bring.
They carry the burden and worry
and can't hear the Bright Angels sing!

Zeus

Zeus in all his might
sends lightning and thunderbolts
to make men cower.

He is angry, hurt
and broken hearted at the
wickedness on Earth.

This was not what he'd
planned or wanted to happen.
Now he takes revenge!

Do Not Make War!

Humans starve animals, children, the sick and poor.
They covet, they steal, they rape and they kill.
Man breaks the 11th Commandment *'Do Not Make War!'*

The Gods in their wisdom gave man their law.
They see him break it, rule by his own will.
Humans starve animals, children, the sick and poor.

Gods come from the Oceans and walk on the shore.
Their hearts full of misery and icy cold chill.
Man breaks the 11th Commandment *'Do Not Make War!'*

Gods glide from the Heavens and stand on the tor.
They stroll in the meadows and bathe in the rill.
Humans starve animals, children, the sick and poor.

Gods rise from the Earths vast boiling core.
See races of men grind Satans stone mill.
Man breaks the 11th Commandment *'Do Not Make War!'*

Gods see the Earth through futures wide door,
when mankind has ravaged and taken its fill.
Humans starve animals, children, the sick and poor.
Man breaks the 11th Commandment *'Do Not Make War!'*

Haiku

Great Ares, wiser
than Mars, stands back and watches
puny humans run.

Elysium

In Heaven the grass is soft and green,
the flowers glow with colours bright,
the ones we love stay close beside
and we're bathed in pure white light.

When we dwell in that enchanted place
a gentle warmth pervades the air,
a million birds sing rapturous songs
and soft winds stir our hair.

Wild animals walk beside the lambs
and sharks swim with the whales,
the wolf packs ties are closely knit
and they roam through Heavens vales.

And in that place are the Devic ones
whose spirits aren't from Earth.
They watch us and they guide us
for they know each humans worth.

And God sits high upon His throne
with a smile for those He greets,
and a cat sits purring on His knee
while a dog lies near His feet.

Haiku

A multi-coloured rainbow
arching high above
the sea, sparkles like hoar frost.

Hellenistic Belle

A lady from ancient Greece
braids her hair, glosses
her nails and wraps her
dress round her like a cloak.

Her slave, little more
than a child, helps her,
and her friend watches.

She has a perfect form,
a perfect face and is
pampered and indulged.

She believes in her true
destiny, knows her place,
allows no-one to touch her.

She is a high priestess,
her word is law and she
dispenses justice cruelly.

Colours

The sun shines,
the lake glows,
the clouds swirl
and farmers work.
Mountains surround,
Angels sing,
the world is happy
and wealth abounds.

Elemental Powers

When God created this wonderful world
with its trees and grass and flowers.
He also made humans with many faults
and wild animals with special powers.

He designed the earth to grow our food,
all His nuts and seeds and fruits,
and the trees that give us shelter
stand firm with ages-old roots.

He taught us how to build a fire
that would protect us all from harm,
would boil our water, cook our food
and keep everyone dry and warm.

He formed the glorious Heavens
with stars and moons and suns.
He gave us air that we might breathe
and glorify all He had done.

Then He gave us magnificent oceans,
and waterfalls, rivers and streams.
He sent rainbows to encircle us
and they glisten in the suns beams.

When we sit outside on a summers day
and smell perfume from flowers and trees,
we know we must strive to keep them safe
or our world might one day cease.

God didn't ask us to destroy His animals,
nor decimate all of His plants.
He placed planet earth into our care,
and nothing, and no-one should want.

Two Haiku

A castle stands strong
in the shadow of Ben More,
and life passes by.

Lochs, glens, mountain mists,
are part of the glory of
Scotland, brave and free.

Dragons

Dragons float through the air on Angels wings,
they dwell in deep caverns,
ride on crests of waves,
soar over the highest mountains,
build castles in the sky.

These magical creatures breathe streams of fire,
protect earthlings from harm,
and will never hurt them.
Their lives are spent fighting
injustice, cruelty and all wrongs.

Exaltation

Egypt - builder of great majesty.
Giant statues of Ramesis sit
where tiny humans visit Abu Simnel
in search of ancient wisdom.

The ruined temple at Philae
is dedicated to the glory of Isis.
It stands, as it always has done,
a monument to perpetual slave labour.

The Sphinx sprawls on her plinth.
What is the enigma of her being,
the wonder of her building,
the silence of her lips of clay?

She rests beside the great pyramid
in all its wondrous splendour.
The oldest known building
in this frantic, callous world.

The boy king called Tutankhamun
did not live long enough to rule.
His impact is in his possessions,
his mummy and his golden death mask.

The temple at Luxor, scene of horror,
is bathed in the mists of antiquity.
Human headed creatures watch warily
the approach of so many alien beings.

Tomb paintings, writings and codes
line the walls of the death chambers.
They depict the life and intrigue
that surrounded the royal courts.

The alabaster mosque of Mohammed Ali
graces the modern skyline,
while a dhow glides silently by
the lush banks of the moonlit Nile.

Volumes Of The Mind

Great books adorn the shelves
of all our libraries.
Some are written in English,
others come from overseas.

We read them, dust them, love them,
perusing every phrase.
Their pages fascinate us,
whether novelettes or plays.

When our stormy day is over
and we hasten to our bed.
We nestle down and read the words
that someone else has said.

Freedoms Voice

I dreamed a dream of happiness and laughter,
of people doing good things every day,
but all my long held hopes were shattered,
for only little children run and play.

Freedoms voice is calling loudly
but I'm locked inside a cage.
I can't walk in scented gardens,
take my place upon earths stage.

My husband revels in his millions,
he shows me off for everyone to see.
I need the right to be my own person,
and live the way I want my life to be.

Freedoms voice is calling loudly
but I'm locked inside a cage.
I can't walk in scented gardens,
take my place upon earths stage.

Two Haiku

Restful, ceaseless sea
whose waters flow forever.
We respect your might.

Cascading water
drops pure and sparkling over
reeds, rocks and small stones.

For All Those Unsung Heroes

Unsung Heroes are people who
give help whenever they can,
to the birds and to the animals,
to a woman, child or man.

They always listen to you
no matter what is wrong,
and your burden gets much lighter
and your spirit becomes strong.

These people often give the
time they cannot really spare,
to help you climb 'Hill Difficulty.'
All your problems they will share.

They don't do this for money
or what's in your bank account.
They do it for love and friendship,
they're the *only* things that count.

Two Haiku

Athena, Goddess
of wisdom, sends the Gorgon
into the dark void.

Neptune, throw me to
the stars. Make my visions true,
lead me to the Gods.

Greek Kalends

Alfred the Great began our navy,
he built ships to guard our coast.
Henry the eighth made it larger
for expansion was his boast.

Canute told the waves to stop,
William wrote the doomsday book.
Richard - called the Lionheart
was famous for the lives he took.

Charles the first was ill-fated
but as a healer he was good,
and even in his own pain
he eased other peoples moods.

When the Merry Monarch reigned
then kindness ruled his court,
and through the plague and fire
his wisdom was often sought.

Now Elizabeth the second rules
and she's had her family troubles.
Like us she's dreamed her dreams,
like us - they've burst her bubbles.

The Monarchy is *our* heritage
it is Englands true intent.
Let's wait until the Greek Kalends
to elect that God-like president!

Heliopolis

Rodos - Island of the Sun God.
Your people shine.
Your country bathes in sunlight.
Olive trees grow abundantly.
Tangerines, oranges, pomegranates, lemons,
all flourish in your rich soil.

Butterflies flutter by.
Golden rays pour down.
Moonbeams thrill the night.
Stars shine in exaltation.
Your land is blest by the Gods.
Apollons Island, Athenas world.

If Only

Let the worlds peoples look to the past
and learn from mistakes made by others.

Let them stop all wars and covetousness.
Let them begin to love their neighbours.
Let them return goodness for evil done to
them and give out more than they receive.

Then the world will not be polluted, poisoned,
over-used. It will smile with sunshine and
bless the enlightened people who inhabit it.

I've Walked That Way Before

Kamiras you're still calling me,
I must visit you once more.
My eyes long to behold you,
I'll come knocking on your door.

Once again I'll tread on stones
where my feet walked 'oft before.
Your ancient streets speak my name
as they did in days of yore.

I'll see my precious house again,
I'll kiss its rough hewn stones.
I'll walk aloft to my own room
where I laid my weary bones.

I'll come to you, you know I will
just as soon as I am able.
No servants now to care for me
or put food upon my table.

I'll walk alone as I know I should,
as you always meant me to.
I'll meditate on planet earth
and what the Gods want me to do.

I'll teach each and every citizen
to be content with what he's got.
Not covet what the others have,
he must join that melting pot.

The pot of all earths animals,
its peoples, fish and birds.
Its insects and its grasses,
its trees and wisdom words.

If we all unite in this good way,
we'll no longer walk alone.
We'll have no wars or starvation,
fights and poverty will have flown.

There are many things I'd like to do
to change our wicked ways,
but one life is just not long enough,
not enough months or weeks or days.

Open Bible

Even Vincent read his Bible
by stubby candlelight.
He opened it in the middle
where the pages all glow bright.

He knew the words of Jesus
and the prophets who are dead.
He was a man of genius
and he was a man well read.

Land Of Milk And Honey

Love is the most powerful emotion.
It can rise up, conquer wars
and starvation.
Cure sicknesses
and open several different doors.

We must love everybody on earth,
no matter what colour their skin,
what religion,
what beliefs.
Only goodness can be allowed in.

We'll have no greed, no avarice,
no desire for other peoples lands,
oil wells,
gold or diamonds.
In friendship we will all join hands.

Utopia, rich land of milk and honey,
animals safe and secure in our arms,
flowers, ferns
and rainforests
flourishing. Earths creatures out of harm.

Haiku

Silently, stars come
peeping through the dark night sky.
They shine down on Earth.

Love Sets You Down On Mars

Love floats you through the stars.
Love yearns with whisp'ring sighs.
Love sets you down on Mars.

Love drives you in fast cars.
Love caresses with his eyes.
Love floats you through the stars.

Love worships you from afar.
Love tells you soulful lies.
Love sets you down on Mars.

Love meets in celestial bars.
Love won't ask you how or why.
Love floats you through the stars.

Love enriches you like a Tsar.
Love infects both girls and guys.
Love sets you down on Mars.

Love deserts and leaves a scar.
Love 'oft times makes you cry.
Love floats you through the stars.
Love sets you down on Mars.

Haiku

I want to go to
Mars. Explore deep caverns and
meet wiser beings.

Mystery, Magic, Fantasy And Dreams

Dragons are mystical beings who have
dwelt on earth throughout all time.
They live in shining silver caves
with Wyverns, Unicorns, Devas and Magi.
They watch over us in our work
and play but we seldom see them.
They help us conquer our fears and
face each new day with hope and joy.

If we are lucky enough to glimpse
one of these glorious creatures,
we'll have earned a great privilege
and the Gods will smile upon us.
We will achieve greatness of spirit
and goodness of soul which will
spread around the world like wildfire,
banishing all dis-ease and hurt.

When Rhiannon leaves her castle
riding the Gold Dragon of Love,
she comes to warn us of impending
disaster, but we listen with deaf ears.
Nobody believes in Fairies and Elves.
Nobody believes in Dragons or Unicorns.
If you open your heart you will hear
the tinkling bells of Angel choirs.

Close the eyes and ears of your body.
See and hear with the soul given you
by the Great Gods. Gather knowledge,
put the Universe to rights. Let all
the Dragons, Wyverns, Fairies, Elves,
Angels, Giants and old time Gods
walk into your hearts and souls.
Create a world where love reigns supreme.

Witchcraft

Witchcraft, Mystery and Magic.
The stuff of Myths and Legends.
Fulfilling dreams, hopes, wishes.

Hedge Witches cure your backaches,
mix potions to find your lover,
pass on the wealth of their wisdom.

White Witches create spells which
help to promote a good life.
This fills your heart with joy.

Beware that Black Satanic crew
who bring bad luck, mishaps, ills.
They make a hellish, potent brew.

Neptunes Kingdom

On Sunday we left Dervaig Bay
to see the Treshnish Isles.
The Puffins were a sheer delight
and we were wreathed in smiles.
Some Shags stood stately on a rock,
wings drying in the sun,
but Razorbills and Guillemots
fought and argued on the run.

We saw a Minke whale that day,
it leapt and dived and blew,
causing great excitement
for the visitors and the crew.

On Monday Neptune favoured us
and Gaias children came,
they performed their antics round our boat
as if we'd called their names.
They were here and there and everywhere
in each place that we looked,
and watching them we felt delight
that for this trip we'd booked.

The awesome grace these creatures have
makes man feel very small,
for he's the great usurper 'tho
he's heard those wild ones call.
They call for help from friends who care,
who want them safe and sound
in one great world-wide sanctuary
where no enemies will be found.

So take your holiday in Dervaig
on the sea-life survey boat,
then you'll help Seals and Porpoises
and Jellyfish that float
around the Scottish Isle of Mull
where all the Dolphins play,
and Basking sharks drift slowly by,
and Whales sing songs each day.

The King Of The Gods

Zeus, king of all the Gods.
Mighty thunderer of the skies.
Three hundred feet he towered above
man with all his puny lies.

The Olympic games were contested
under His auspicious eye,
where naked athletes tried their skills
and chariots round the track didst fly.

Costly gifts to the temples were brought
and priests performed their awesome rites.
Each athlete desired to be supreme
and paid the Gods to grant him might.

Queen Of The Snow Kingdom

The Snow Queen with her creatures
walking round her feet,
sees the wondrous mountains
and the Valkyries vast fleet.

She transports to her castle
with pennants flying high
and nods to Heavens host
in the dark vaults of the sky.

Her wisdom is all-knowing,
her robe's a perfect blue
and the whiteness of the snow
gilds the clouds with ghostly hue.

This woman is not mortal,
she's not made of flesh and blood,
she is true ethereal beauty
like a rose that's just in bud.

Two Haiku

Dragons float on clouds,
crystal castles drift slowly,
Devas ride the winds.

The stars shine above.
The moon glows with spectral light.
God smiles upon us.

Ocean Life

Golden sand, gilded by orange and yellow
as the suns rays softly touch the beach.
Little waves ripple gently, and rock pools,
so full of life, are suddenly out of reach.

The water, green, purple and aquamarine,
races with white foamy crests to the shore.
It covers the shifting shingle and shells
which carpet the oceans vast floors.

The whales, the dolphins and fishes
live their lives in the briny seas,
and seabirds float on top of the waves
while yachts sail along in the breeze.

Some mermaids swim with the dolphins
and sea-horses talk to the whales,
while Neptune guards his castle from
sea-dragons with long lashing tails.

And Poseidon pursues Polybites,
and pins him to the oceans deep,
and Nisiros bubbles and puffs
from the giants ages-old sleep.

For the oceans are full of magic
and magic is what you will see,
every time that you go to the seashore
or sail over that beautiful sea.

Our Gods Have Changed, It's True

Our Gods have changed, it's true.
George Bush, Colin Powell, Tony Blair.
They've elevated themselves to an elite few.

These new Gods take a very narrow view
of anyone else's thoughts or cares.
Our Gods have changed, it's true.

They bomb, burn, break, smash and hew
their way into other countries affairs.
They've elevated themselves to an elite few.

Donald Rumsfeld is part of that crew
and Jack Straw also takes his share.
Our Gods have changed, it's true.

The glory boys, masonic, red and blue
are full of their own importance and flair.
They've elevated themselves to an elite few.

They'll destroy the world, we'll all rue
the day we voted them into power chairs.
Our Gods have changed, it's true.
They've elevated themselves to an elite few.

Haiku

Mars, bringer of war,
sees mankinds greed and envy
while Emperors fight.

Shimmering Water

The water shimmers, glowing blue and green.
Ripples gently spread across the lake
and rainbow colours softly gild the sheen.

A boat drifts aimlessly through the scene
and a man trails his fingers, only half awake.
The water shimmers, glowing blue and green.

Swans flap wings, wash feathers, preen.
The man watches some ducks with a drake
and rainbow colours softly gild the sheen.

Rich, lustrous flora and fauna can be seen,
and a Fairy, ethereal like a melting snowflake.
The water shimmers, glowing blue and green.

His spirit is ready to fight evil. To clean
all injustices from this planet for loves sake,
and rainbow colours softly gild the sheen.

His wifes death, cruel men, vicious, mean.
He must return home, end his grief-stricken wake.
The water shimmers, glowing blue and green
and rainbow colours softly gild the sheen.

Haiku

Waterfalls cascade
down mountainsides and tumble
over rocks and shrubs.

Space Fantasy

The moon shines in the Heavens above
with planets and stars surrounding.
She lights a path through the dark hours
with bright silver beams abounding.

So much beauty, so many colours
hold this great Universe in sway.
Millions of gentle, sentient beings
are trillions of light years away.

If they came here, would we greet them
with hands outstretched as friends,
or experiment on their living bodies,
feeling pleasure as their lives end.

We wouldn't be able to love them,
we humans are violent and brash,
so God help another worlds space ships
if on earth they should ever crash!

Valhalla

The Gods watch from Valhalla
where all dead heroes dwell.
Odin, Thor, Balder and Loki
guard well their magic spells
from man who walks the earth
in these present troubled times,
for he has damaged everything,
has shamed his youth and prime.

Stonehenge

Stonehenge, Mystery, Enchantment.
What is the reason of your being?
What magic key are you holding?
Why were you built and what acts
of violence took place long aeons ago?

Were there rough druidical tortures?
Did young boys scream and die?
Are your ancient stones still bloody
from the things they saw and felt,
the cries - the tears - the woes.

Have we learnt? Are we any better?
Do we honour and care for all creatures?
Do we love, help and cherish,
or do we throw our short lives away
to the Devil waiting in the wings?

Malapert
(Impudent, Saucy)

A black cat sits like an Egyptian statue.
A tabby crouches with eyes narrowed,
their whiskers twitch expectantly,
their tails curl round their bodies.

Such beauty - such peace - such joy,
wild things yet purringly tame,
soft fur - pointed ears - shining coats,
perfect felines - glorious creatures.

Sunshine Meadows

A little bird high in the sky.
A golden-yellow butterfly.
Some lilac wafting in the breeze
and soft winds whisp'ring through the trees.

The lawn mown in the month of May
smells fresh as on a summers day.
The sky's pale blue and fluffy clouds
glide o'er the parks gay chattering crowds.

The sun shines down on earthly life,
on animals, children, man and wife.
The blossoms swirl, the insects pass
and naked feet run through the grass.

Then happiness shines out over all
who listen to that birds sweet call,
as he chirps at every break of day
and at evening 'ere he glides away.

Great love flows out from dogs and cats,
whose joy's fulfilled by gentle pats
and walks in woods where sunshine beams,
and drinks from tiny rippling streams.

For peace reigns in the summertime
when winter's gone and all's sublime
and sunshine turns our hearts around
to pastures where true love is found.

The Gods Come

The Gods come. They are, they exist.
From Northern fields to Valhallas halls.
They float through diaphanous mist.

In warmer climes, by soft winds kis't.
Meccas women wearing Allahs shawls.
The Gods come. They are, they exist.

The Indian hierarchy, a diffuse list.
Women in saris weave Lord Krishnas palls.
They float through diaphanous mist.

The Celts, warlike with a Bardic twist.
Matriarchal systems, Rhiannons falls.
The Gods come. They are, they exist.

The Great Olympian Gods made a tryst
with mankind, bound by Zeus' walls.
They float through diaphanous mist.

Angels, Archangels and Fairies are grist
to the mills of Heaven. The Great God calls.
The Gods come. They are, they exist.
They float through diaphanous mist.

Haiku

Thor, hammer held high
surveys the Earthlings struggles
and yearns to help them.

The Gods Of War

From Ramesis to Xerxes, Darius, Alexander,
leaders have sought to expand their empires,
and consigned countless millions to bondage.

Since Julius, Atilla, Charlemagne, Bloodaxe,
man has desired another nations wealth,
their lands, their lives, their freedoms.

From Richard to Henry, Napoleon, Hitler,
they've tortured, gassed, killed, scarred,
in order to feed their innate power lust.

Aeons later Bush, Blair and cronies
use tearing, shattering, awesome bombs.
No one ever heeds what history teaches.

The whole world is tottering in deadly peril,
much worse than ever before. Bush and Blair
march on towards their ugly space in hell.

Insatiable greed urges man to go to war.
We can only pray the Gods grant us all a
measure of peace, freedom and serenity,
in spite of a thousand crazed warlords.

Haiku

Odin, tied upside
down to the tree Ygdrasil,
learns Runic meanings.

The Woman Shivers In Winters Chill

In a thatched cottage beside a rill
with Christmas roses above the door.
The woman shivers in winters chill.

She writes her memoirs with a quill,
reminiscing on days of yore.
In a thatched cottage beside a rill.

Remembering the man she had to kill
when her father fought in the war.
The woman shivers in winters chill.

She dreams of her lover and the thrill,
holding him close, needing him more.
In a thatched cottage beside a rill.

Huddling by the fire quiet and still,
with the bird of bright feathers she soars.
The woman shivers in winters chill.

Deaths Dark Angel crosses the sill,
but the old woman has gone before.
In a thatched cottage beside a rill
The woman shivers in winters chill.

Haiku

The twinkling stars and planets
gild the Heavens on
dark, cold December evenings.

The Land That I Hold Dear

England - Rose flower of the sea.
Ever staunchant - ever free.
Greenest Isle with golden beaches
girded round by watery reaches.

Wondrous land of hills and dales,
all other countries beauty pales
beside your own, your crags and tors,
and blueish-purple heathered moors.

Your counties, each and every one,
are pearls beneath the pallid sun
that shines out over your great land,
carved long ago by Natures hand.

She made a thousand little dells
and carpeted them with blue harebells.
She fashioned little country lanes
and churches topped by weather vanes.

She ordered little tinkly streams
to flow where lovers sit and dream,
and bridges cross the waterfalls
where dippers and kingfishers call.

She made the wildlife and the flowers,
and cosy, leafy, fairy bowers.
She placed her colours in the sky
where white and fluffy clouds roll by.

While nations come and nations go
and rivers down tall mountains flow,
this English Isle in all its glory
writes its own inimitable story.

Vikings

Cruising can be fun but
it can be a form of hell.
Rolling waves,
rocking boats
as any sailor could tell.

The Vikings came in longships,
crossed freezing, northern seas.
Woollen sails
drove them on,
strong hardy men were these.

I wonder how they managed,
I guess many of them died.
Cold and sneezes,
rheumatism?
Yet thousands of them tried.

Haiku

The handsome Balder,
slain by pure white mistletoe,
looks down with kindness.

Voodoo

Beware the urban witch-doctor
for he owns a motley lot
of animal skins and skeletons
which he puts into his pot.

He stirs his magic potion
which he says will do you good,
but the animals that are in it
are not your type of food.

He kills endangered species
without sorrow or a thought
of the things that he has given you
in the magic you have bought.

He preys on simple people
who believe in all he's said.
He takes money that they can't afford
for the poisons he has bred.

So stamp down hard upon him,
don't let him through your door,
don't listen to his chatter,
just tell him he's a bore!

Don't let him make his fortune
from the money you have spent,
for the evil things that he has done
make him one unpleasant gent!

Walking With Nightmares

The Vampires of our nightly dreams
show us the causes of their schemes.
Mans arguments black out the beams
the Gods send down in golden streams.

Great Allosaurs chase up the hill
humans who daily break Gods will,
they can't escape Satans cold chill
until their hearts with kindness fill.

And Lions hunt and Tigers bite
all through the day and into the night.
The Wolf stays low, he will not fight
but knows that mankind is not right!

Bright Dragons float and Unicorns
with magic in their long curled horns,
seek to remove mankinds dark thorn
placed in his side when he was born.

Cast out dark thoughts and glow with love,
then watch the stars shine up above,
lose the gauntlet, don silver gloves,
let your soul be pure as the gentle dove.

Water Carrier

The aquarian age rushed headlong in,
most people think that is great,
but to me it's just hocus-pocus,
not kismet, karma or fate!

Alternative medicine's all the rage
but it's dreadfully expensive,
poor people can't afford it
and the NHS gets defensive.

Our drugs cost lots of money
and they don't do us much good,
they can't combat the additives
put into our drinks and food.

We are in a terrible mess now
'twixt the devil and deep blue sea,
but there *is* something better,
and that thing's totally free.

Go and visit a spiritual healer
when your life is in a mess,
they'll get you back in shape,
heal all your ills and stress.

They won't talk about the new age,
won't bore you with their ideas,
they'll try to help you feel good,
cure your backaches and your fears.

Zenith

The Midnight Sun - fantastic!
In freezing polar waters.
Orange - yellow - gigantic.

Humankind is awed, ecstatic,
and leaves its cosy quarters.
The Midnight Sun - fantastic!

In the north sea and atlantic
Kelpies tempt your daughters.
Orange - yellow - gigantic.

The Banshees wail is frantic,
it makes many strong men falter.
The Midnight Sun - fantastic!

Iormungards anger's erratic,
the great waves are his altar.
Orange - yellow - gigantic.

Ragnarok's excessively drastic.
Wolf Fenrir's lost his halter.
The Midnight Sun - fantastic!
Orange - yellow - gigantic.

Haiku

Majestic Mountains, Misty Seas,
Norway in all its splendour,
its beauty will never cease.

The World Of Men!

We're going to have identity
cards just like in the war.
Next it will be ration books
with queuing at the doors.

Our lives are on a microchip
which is hidden from our sight.
The ten year census adds to this,
it increases parliaments might!

We're told the census isn't seen,
yet the figures from it are used
to calculate schools and hospitals,
do you think we're being abused?

We'll stand in line, ankles chained,
never allowed to do our own thing.
No access to a telephone, no freedom
and nothing to make our hearts sing.

They'll 'ear'ole' everything we say.
They'll follow us home from work.
We'll never have truth or privacy.
They already treat us like jerks!

Nineteen eighty four was close,
they had started bugging us then,
now it's getting much, much worse.
This is the world of men!